HERBS

HERBS

A QUANTUM BOOK

Published by Grange Books
an imprint of Grange Books Plc
The Grange
Kingsnorth Industrial Estate
Hoo, nr. Rochester
Kent ME3 9ND

ISBN 1-84013-139-X

This book is produced by
Quantum Books Ltd
6 Blundell Street
London N7 9BH

Project Manager: Rebecca Kingsley
Project Editor: Judith Millidge
Design/Editorial: David Manson
Andy McColm, Maggie Manson

The material in this publication previously appeared in
*The Book of Herbs, The Complete Book of Herbs,
The Herb Handbook*

QUMAFH
Set in Futura
Reproduced in Singapore by Eray Scan
Printed in Singapore by Star Standard Industries (Pte) Ltd

Contents

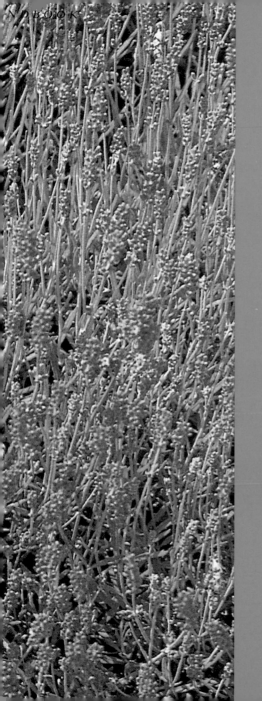

THE HUMBLE HEALER

Growing herbs is one of the most delightful aspects of gardening. The plants are pleasantly fragrant, mostly decorative, some are very colourful, and the majority have uses in the kitchen or around the home. Added to that, herbs are among the easiest of plants to grow, making them an ideal springboard for the new and inexperienced gardener.

Herbs through History

People have made use of herbs since the beginning of time. In the past, not only were herbs both food and medicine, but they were also important in religious rites and festivals with many superstitions surrounding them.

ROMAN HERBS

The Romans made such lavish use of herbs in both medicines and cooking that the plants were a vital part of the equipment of the advancing Roman armies. The use of herbs in all the once colonised countries of Europe can be traced back directly to the Romans.

MONASTIC HERBS

Herbal uses declined with the Roman Empire, to re-emerge in the monasteries of the Middle Ages. The monks put herbs to both medicinal and culinary use and eventually their knowledge spread allowing people to grow their own self-help remedies.

Left. A walled herb garden in the style of a monastery of the Middle Ages.

Above. A patio container planted with basil, parsley and chives.

HERBAL LITERATURE

During the 16th century, many books were published setting out the healing properties and uses of herbs. Nicholas Culpeper's *Herball* identified the medicinal herbal plants and defined their uses. He was a follower of a form of natural healing known as the Doctrine of Signatures, which teaches that 'like cures like'. In other words, red flowers, for example, are most likely to cure disorders of the blood.

HERBAL REVIVAL

By the 19th century, the use of herbs had again fallen into decline. Indeed, until recently, parsley, thyme, mint and chives were the only herbs that were in most gardens. However, now the pendulum has swung back and herbs are at the centre of a strong organic revival. People have rediscovered the advantages of growing natural produce and herbs are being used in many increasingly imaginative ways.

Planning a Herb Garden

Planning a herb garden is the first exciting stage in a continuing process that may become a fascinating hobby. Whether you have a large herb garden, or a few simple patio pots and planters growing herbs will be, before long, a fulfilling, rewarding pastime.

FIND A SUNNY SPOT

Most herbs originate in the sunny climate of the Mediterranean and so you need to find a sunny spot. Herbs probably require 5–6 hours of sunshine each day, although there are a few shade-loving herbs which are found in the directory section (see p.16). These can be planted in the shadow of taller trees, or beside a wall or fence.

HERBS NEAR THE HOUSE

You can still grow herbs in colder regions, if you choose a sheltered spot and erect a windbreak. Try to pick a site close to a window, so that the scent of the plants can waft into the house. This also means that, on a rainy day, it is easier to gather a few herb leaves without wearing rubber boots and a raincoat!

Left. Gather herbs in the morning when their fragrance is strongest .

Above. Colourful flowers and contrasting leaves make for a lively border.

PLANNING AND MIXING

It is a good idea to draw a scale plan of your garden, drawing in any existing or proposed paths and then allocating the space for the herbs you choose. The details in the directory section giving the possible height and growing tips for each plant will be helpful in deciding which herbs will fit in. Try to make your choice a mixture of those herbs you will use in the kitchen, and others that may be colourful and which may also attract bees to the garden.

COLOUR AND TEXTURE

Take not only height and width but also colour and texture into consideration as you build up your plan, and create exciting visual effects by blending silver-leaved plants with purple leaves; yellow leaves with dark green; matt leaves with glossy eaves; plain leaves beside ferny leaves. In this way each of your herbs can be seen at its most pleasing and each will draw attention to it's neighbour. A herb garden doesn't have to be all green!

11

Growing Herbs

Soil is *the* significant source of food and water for herbs. The way you prepare the ground will have a major effect on the health and quality of your plants for years to come, so it is well worth taking a little time and trouble at this stage.

PREPARING THE SOIL

Good soil is essential for most plants, although there are a few plants that will flourish even in undernourished, poor quality soil. Most herbs have a common dislike of sitting in damp soil with permanently wet roots, so good drainage is essential. If water does not sink in, your soil has too much clay. If the soil remains only wet on top, then it is too sandy.

ACIDITY AND ALKALINITY

Most herbs like a neutral or slightly alkaline soil around pH 6.0–7.5. pH is a numerical measure of acid and alkali, with 0 the most acidic, 14 the most alkaline and 7 being neutral. Simple kits for pH testing are available at garden centres. If the soil test shows your soil is too acidic, then you can amend the pH and make it more alkaline by digging in some lime with humus.

SOWING SEEDS IN POTS

1. Put in a layer of broken crocks at the bottom of the pot, then loosely fill with soil.

2. Sow the seeds thinly to avoid too much crowding when the seedlings appear.

3. Sprinkle a thin layer of soil to cover the seeds and keep them moist.

4. Use a fine sprinkler for watering. Cover the pot with glass and keep warm.

STARTING FROM SCRATCH

If you are starting a herb garden from scratch you should first dig it over to a depth of 30cm (12in). This is the comfortable depth achieved with a garden spade. Dig in a layer of peat or compost to improve the aeration of the soil. This helps improve drainage in clay soils and helps to hold water in sandy soils.

PLANTS OR SEEDS

You must decide whether to buy nursery-grown plants or seeds. Planting seeds is quick and easy. You plant in pots, or trays, water well and seedlings appear in a few days (see step-by-step above). However, you may prefer the appeal of the 'instant' garden and opt to buy plants from a garden centre or nursery.

Using Herbs

With a few pots of herbs on a windowsill, a tub of contrasting herbs on a balcony, or a small plot devoted to aromatic plants, fragrance is at your fingertips for cooking, health and decoration.

COOKING WITH HERBS

Sometimes it is a single herb that does most to complement a dish; basil with tomato; rosemary with roast lamb; summer savoury with green beans; sage and onion stuffing with turkey. At other times, a partnership of herbs is more traditional. Whatever the combination, a collection of herbs to be used as condiments is the single most beneficial weapon in a cook's armoury.

HEALTH AND BEAUTY HERBS

Lemon verbena tea can be helpful for insomnia; valerian to settle nerves; sage to treat sore throats and other winter ills; hyssop for gargling; calendula for broken skin; check the directory (see p.16) for the many medical herbal uses. Herbal oils are popular in aromatherapy and massage, while herbal vinegars can be added to the rinsing water after washing hair or clothes.

DECORATIVE AROMATIC HERBS

Even if they had no culinary, medical or cosmetic applications, many herbs would be grown for their decorative and aromatic properties alone. Bunches of marjoram and tansy flowers hanging in a corner, a pot of fresh herb leaves on a kitchen table, evergreen herbs bound to a twig ring or a dish of fragrant pot pourri to scent a living room or bedroom. Herbs have a lot to offer in terms of good looks and pleasing aroma.

Above. This medley of aromatic herbs is arranged over bands of lavender flowers and pot pourri.

Pot pourri is a delightful way of preserving herbs in a decorative and aromatic way. Choose some flowers for their appearance and some for their perfume. Gather leaves as much for their shape and colour as for their aroma. A blend of different fragrances will provide a fresh herbal aroma in your home.

15

HERB SPECIES

Key to symbols
A number of icons are used in the directory to describe the uses of each specific herb. These are explained below.

Culinary

Healing

Cosmetics

Scented

Decorative

Warning!

<u>THROUGHOUT THE DIRECTORY</u>
The botanical name for the species is given first in alphabetical order, followed by common names.

ACHILLEA MILLEFOLIUM YARROW

Common yarrow grows as a rampant weed in fields and hedgerows, where it varies from a low creeping form to a tough plant. Other forms (*A.millefolium v. rosea* and *A. filipendulina*, respectively) have pink-and-cream or bright yellow flowers.

Features Flat headed-flowers.
Colour White.
Height 60cm (2ft).
Growing tips Full sun or shade, any soil.
Uses Leaves in salads, on wounds, for greasy skin, washing hair.

ACONITUM NAPELLUS MONKSHOOD

A highly poisonous plant which has been used as a healing plant for centuries. A garden perennial with distinctive leaves. Each root lasts only a year and all parts of the features are used; the top growth is collected in summer and the root in autumn.

Features Flowers in mid-summer.
Colour Deep rich blue flowers.
Height 60cm (2ft).
Growing tips Slow to establish from seed—use a daughter tuber for success.
Uses Only prescribed under medical supervision due to its toxicity.

ALLIUM SATIVUM GARLIC

A member of the onion family, the
garlic bulb is an indispensable
flavouring in cooking. The cloves may
be white, pink or purple skinned and
the number and flavour vary
considerably between varieties.

Features Bulb encased in a paper
case.
Colour Pink or white flowerhead.
Height 60cm (2ft).
Growing tips Best in well-drained
soil in a sunny position.
Uses In cooking. Added to olive oil
to flavour it. As an antiseptic, cold
remedy and a diuretic.

ALLIUM SCHOENOPRASUM CHIVES

A member of the onion family, grown
from bulbs, they have a delicate,
onion-like flavour and are widely used
in cooking. Cultivated since the 16th
century. Used in egg and cheese dishes
and as a garnish.

Features Clumps of grass-like leaves.
Colour Deep-mauve or pink heads in
mid-summer.
Height 23cm (9in).
Growing tips Flourish in moist,
well-drained soil, in partial shade.
Also do well in pots.
Uses Sprinkled on salads, on soups
and meat. Leaves are slightly antiseptic.

ALOYSIA TRIPHYLLA LEMON VERBENA

Lemon verbena has a strong citrus aroma that is at its best in early evening. It thrives in hot climates and does well at the back of a sunny border. It is hardy but can need winter protection in cool areas.

Features Perennial, deciduous shrub.
Colour Pale purple flowers in late summer.
Height 1.5m (5ft).
Growing tips Grow from seed or soft cuttings.
Uses Flavouring stuffings, fruit salads, soft drinks. Pot pourri, mild sedative.

ALTHAEA OFFICINALIS ENGLISH MALLOW

A member of the hollyhock family, the mucilage, almost 30% of the roots, was used to make marshmallow. The five-petalled flowers are saucer shaped, and bloom in late summer.

Features Small attractive flowers carried without stems.
Colour White or pink flowers.
Height 1.2m (4ft).
Growing tips Prefers damp, keep moist in dry summers.
Uses Shredded for soups and salads, the roots fried in butter. Sprains, mouthwash and bruises.

ANETHUM GRAVEOLENS DILL

This hardy annual yields two culinary components, its seeds and its feathery leaves, which are known as dill weed. The green stem carries large flat umbellifers of bright yellow flowers that bloom in mid-summer.

Features Ultra-fine, feathery leaves.
Colour Bright yellow flowers.
Height 75cm (30in).
Growing tips Sow where it will be grown as it does not transplant well.
Uses Leaves used in salads, fish dishes and sauces. Seed oil used in making gripe water.

ANGELICA ARCHANGELICA ANGELICA

A giant member of the parsley family, it grows in many parts of the world. Its name is thought to come from the feast day of St Michael the Archangel, May 8, when the plant flowers.

Features Aromatic plant with fleshy roots, thick, hollow stems, huge leaves.
Colour Small yellowish-green flowers.
Height 1.5m (5ft).
Growing tips Only grown from seed in moist soil in late summer, early winter.
Uses Fleshy stems are candied for cake decorations, leaves for flavouring, oil in gin, pot pourri. Flatulence, colds and appetite stimulant.

ANTHEMIS NOBILIS CHAMOMILE

A perennial plant of the composite family, it is one of the daintiest herbs. There is a non-flowering variety, Treneague, which is used for lawns.

Features Apple scented.
Colour Daisy-like, creamy white flowers with yellow conical centres.
Height 30cm (1ft).
Growing tips Easy to grow from the division of runners and from seed.
Uses Dispepsia, flatulence, mild antiseptic. Infusion of dried flowers used as a rinse for fair hair and as a skin tonic.

ANTHRISCUS CEREFOLIUM CHERVIL

Closely related to parsley, chervil is one of the classic herbs used in French cooking, particularly omelettes. It is a hardy annual, easy to grow but quickly goes to seed. Use fresh for best flavour.

Features Fern-like leaves with a slight aniseed aroma.
Colour White flowers in mid-summer.
Height 50cm (20in).
Growing tips Easily grown from seed in a planter or window box. It prefers moist, shady positions.
Uses Flavoured butter, soup garnish, egg and cheese dishes.

ARMORACIA RUSTICANA HORSERADISH

The classic accompaniment to roast beef, the large fleshy roots are strongly aromatic. Like raw onions they make your eyes water as you prepare them. This perennial plant has been used as a flavouring for at least 3,000 years.

Features Long, thick, fleshy roots covered by a rough and hairy brown skin.
Colour Tiny white flowers.
Height 50cm (20in).
Growing tips An avid coloniser, so restraint is needed. Thrives anywhere.
Uses Mix with cream, in sauces for meat and fish.

ARTEMISIA ABSINTHIUM WORMWOOD

This is one of the most magical plants of the herb garden. Primarily a flavouring for liqueurs and aperitifs because of its unique fragrance. Dappled shade or full sunshine are suitable, but they appreciate some shelter from strong winds.

Features Rounded bush with pale green, deeply cut leaves which are silvery when young.
Colour Green-yellow flowers in summer.
Height 120cm (4ft).
Growing tips Propagate from summer cuttings or seed and protect in winter.
Uses Pot pourri and herb sachets, essential oil.

ARTEMISIA ABROTANUM SOUTHERNWOOD

A bushy shrub grown, in informal gardens and herbaceous borders, as a decorative and strongly aromatic plant, said to be repellant to bees. The leaves are strong and feathery, deep grey-green in colour.

Features Feathery, pungent leaves.
Colour Tiny yellow flowers in summer.
Height 90cm (3ft).
Growing tips A rich soil and sunny position is needed. Protect in winter.
Uses Has been used as a flavouring. The dried plant can be used as an antiseptic and a stimulant. A yellow dye can be extracted from the stems.

ARTEMISIA DRACUNCULUS TARRAGON

French, as opposed to Russian tarragon, has a more subtle flavour, pale leaves and a bitter taste. The hardy perennial originates from Southern Europe.

Features Leaves are long, slender, pointed and a rich dark green.
Colour Lime green clusters of flowers.
Height 2.4m (8ft).
Growing tips Grow from a piece of rhizome in spring or cuttings in summer.
Uses Must be used sparingly due to its distinctive flavour. Use in chicken, white fish, egg and cheese recipes.

ATROPA BELLADONNA BELLADONA

Now a rare perennial cultivated in specialist collections, though once plentiful in the countryside. It is a powerful narcotic, well known for its poisonous qualities and used in homeopathic medicine.

Features Large oval pointed leaves grow in pairs and cherry-like berries.
Colour Dingy purple-brown flowers.
Height 1.5m (5ft).
Growing tips Alkaline soil in dappled shade is required.
Uses Use only under medical supervision. Not to be handled if cuts or abrasions on the hands.

BORAGO OFFICINALIS BORAGE

This hardy annual has an untidy, straggling habit but the flowers make this one of the prettiest of herb plants. The leaves have no fragrance and are unremarkable. The plant self-seeds and will colonise a large area.

Features Star-shaped flowers and cucumber flavoured leaves.
Colour Light blue, star-shaped flowers.
Height 45cm (18in).
Growing tips Easy to grow from seed sown outdoors in spring.
Uses Traditional decoration for gin-based cocktails, garnish, cake decoration. Infusions for coughs.

BRASSICA JUNCEA MUSTARD

This is a brown mustard suitable for modern harvesting. Grown indoors, mustard can be eaten at the cotyledon stage, as a salad.

Features Essential oil forms when dry powder is mixed with water.
Colour Yellow four-petalled flowers.
Height 1.5m (5ft).
Growing tips May be grown outdoors from seed in spring, in moist soil and a sunny position.
Uses Added to salad dressings, egg and cheese dishes. The seed is a preservative used in pickling. Mix with hot water to relax feet.

CALAMINTHA NEPETOIDES CALAMINTHA

A small, erect, bushy little plant grown for its aromatic foliage reminiscent of the scent of thyme. Mainly used to relieve flatulence.

Features Aromatic foliage.
Colour Whitish-mauve tiny flowers.
Height 60cm (2ft).
Growing tips Plant division, cuttings in spring and seed are ways to propagate in dryish, alkaline soil.
Uses Used for liver and spleen trouble, cramp, shortness of breath, as a contraceptive and with salt, to clear worms.

CALENDULA OFFICINALIS MARIGOLD

A hardy annual, the plant is a native of southern Europe but flourishes in cool, temperate climates. Once treasured for its culinary uses, the fresh or dried petals have been used as a saffron substitute since Roman times.

Features Daisy-shaped flowers.
Colour Brilliant yellow or orange.
Height 23cm (9in).
Growing tips Rich, light soil in a sunny position, readily self-seeds.
Uses Petals used in soups, rice dishes and a colouring for cheese. The petals used to heal wounds and treat conjunctivitis, wasp and bee stings.

CARUM CARVI CARAWAY

A biennial grown commercially for its seed in northern Europe, the United States, and North Africa. At its most effective when grown as a clump.

Features A straggly plant with delicate clusters of flowers and feathery leaves.
Colour Clusters of white flowers tinged with pink.
Height 60cm (2ft).
Growing tips Good soil, partial shade for seeds sown outdoors in early autumn.
Uses Leaves in salads and soups, the seeds in baking cheese and meat dishes. Used as an aid for digestion.

CHRYSANTHEMUM BALSAMITA ALECOST

Originally from the Middle East, this plant was taken to America in the 17th century by colonists and now grows along roadsides. The leaves are green and have a light bloom. In America it goes by the name of Bible leaf as it was used as a Bible marker.

Features Slight balsam-mint aroma.
Colour Small, yellow button-like flowers in July.
Height 90cm (3ft).
Growing tips Sow seed in a sunny position in spring.
Uses Salads, with game and cold meats, pot pourri, nosegay sachets.

CHRYSANTHEMUM PARTHENIUM FEVERFEW

This is a year-round decorative garden plant. Low growing, bushy, vigorous and self-seeding. The flowers dry well for flower arranging and the bright lime green or yellowy-green leaves, retain their colour through the winter.

Features Pungent, bitter leaves and daisy-like small flowers.
Colour White daisy-like flowers.
Height 60cm (2ft).
Growing tips Thrives in the poorest soils, even in paving cracks and walls.
Uses Fresh or dry leaves are effective as a cure for migraine and as a tonic.

CONVALLARIA MAJALIS LILY OF THE VALLEY

Richly scented, the plant is indigenous to lowlands, especially wooded areas. The creeping rhizomes form colonies with spear-like leaves and flowers, which appear in late spring.

Features Can be forced in pots for indoor decoration.
Colour White, dangling bell flowers.
Height 20cm (8in).
Growing tips Moisture-rich soil and shade.
Uses Pot pourri. Dried powdered flowers claimed to relieve nasal mucus, vertigo ear inflammation.

CORIANDRUM SATIVUM CORIANDER

Coriander seed is mentioned in the Bible but goes back much further in time. It has been used both in cooking and medicine for thousands of years, and is a hardy annual.

Features Feathery leaves and spherical seeds are used in the kitchen.
Colour Small white flowers.
Height 60cm (2ft).
Growing tips Easy to grow in light, well-drained soil in plenty of sun.
Uses Frozen leaves used in curries, roast lamb covering, salads, chutney. Roasted seeds used in sausages, curries, casseroles, pickling spice.

DATURA STRAMONIUM THORN APPLE

Known in America as Jimson or
Jamestown weed as this was the first
area where it became established. Very
rare in Great Britain, only found in
wasteland. A large coarse herb with
strongly veined leaves with a wavy
tooth margin.

Features Long tubular flowers with
seed capsules resembling green
gooseberries with numerous spines.
Colour White trumpet-shaped flowers.
Height 1.2m (4ft).
Growing tips Very poor quality soil
for seed sewn in spring.
Uses Seed tincture used for asthma.

DIANTHUS CARYOPHYLLUS PINK

A familiar and pretty cottage-garden
plant which grows wild in southern
Europe and India. A clove substitute
in the past.

Features Delicately coloured, they
are ideal edging for a herb garden.
Colour Single or clustered pink, red,
crimson or white.
Height 60cm (2ft).
Growing tips Can be sewn from
seed but more usually propagated by
root division.
Uses Flavour syrups, fruit salads,
jellies, fruit drinks. Pot pourri.

DICTAMNUS ALBUS FRAXINELLA

The drug extracted from the root bark is little known today, but was used against scrofulous diseases. Also known as the burning bush, it has a volatile oil in the leaves which vaporises in heat and can be set alight. The flames dance around the plant leaving it unharmed.

Features Rich balsamic lemon scent of flowers and leaves.
Colour White flowers.
Height 60cm (2ft).
Growing tips Best in full sunshine, in a fertile, dampish loam.
Uses Lemon scent of oil.

DIGITALIS PURPUREA FOXGLOVE

No synthetic drug has replaced the cardiac glycosides that are obtainable from the foxglove. It is of immense importance in medicine and essential in the physic garden. One of the most poisonous plants of the British flora, it is a true biennial.

Features Large wrinkled leaves.
Colour Purple-red bell shaped flowers.
Height 2m (7ft).
Growing tips Easy to culivate from seed and self-seedling once fully established.
Uses Cardiac medicines.

ERYNGIUM MARITIMUM SEA HOLLY

Looking like a thistle, the sea holly is a spiny plant with undulating leaves, each curve ending in a fearsome spine. A perennial that used to be a common sight on beaches and sand dunes.

Features Spiked leaves.
Colour Steely blue flowers.
Height 45cm (18in).
Growing tips Easy to grow in good garden soil in a sunny position. Good drainage encourages roots to grow.
Uses Eryngo root is added to jams, jellies, and candied as a sweetmeat. The aromatic roots are used as a cough sweet, nerve tonic and diuretic.

EUPATORIUM PURPUREUM JO PYE WEED

Named after an Indian medicine man in New England, who cured typhus fever with this plant. The medicinal value lies in its roots. A common meadow weed from Canada to Florida.

Features Flowers late in summer and good for the back of borders.
Colour Rose-purple fluffy flowers.
Height 1.5m (5ft).
Growing tips Dampish soil needed. Divide the clumps in autumn.
Uses In medicine, to treat urinary disorders, gout and rheumatism as it is a strong diuretic.

FRAGARIA VESCA WILD STRAWBERRY

The true wild strawberry provides sweet deep red fruits in mid-summer. Long runners root at intervals to form new plants and the lower leaves form a rosette.

Features Attractive to let run among paving slabs and dry walls.
Colour Red fruits and white flowers.
Height 30cm (1ft).
Growing tips Sow seed in pots or boxes and plant out as tiny plants. Replace the mother plant each autumn.
Uses Fruit salads, compotes, cheese-cake decoration or rich cold meats.

FOENICULUM VULGARE FENNEL

Fennel leaves have an anise-like flavour. The plant is a hardy perennial and likes well-drained soil and a sunny position. It is a native of southern Europe and used by the Romans.

Features Soft thread-like leaves.
Colour Pale pink to white.
Height 1.5m (5ft).
Growing tips Seed may be sewn in place in spring, and thinned out or existing plants increased by root division.
Uses Leaves used with pork, fish, sauces and stuffings. Seeds used as a spice. For flatulence and gripe water.

FRAGARIA/FOENICULUM

GENTIANA LUTES YELLOW GENTIAN

The yellow gentian was introduced to Britain from Europe. It is a statuesque plant holding itself poker straight. The leaves, in pairs, clasp the stem to form cups which are filled with starry flowers.

Features An upright plant with roots that plunge 1m (3ft) into the ground.
Colour Golden yellow starry flowers.
Height 1.5m (5ft).
Growing tips Can be grown from seed but root cuttings are the more usual method.
Uses Roots used as an appetite stimulant, the bruised leaves make an antiseptic dressing.

GLECHOMA HEDERACEA GROUND IVY

This plant runs across the ground, rooting as it progresses. It remains green all the year unless there is a severe frost. The plant is common on wasteland, particulary on damp, heavy soils.

Features Attracts butterflies and suppresses weeds.
Colour Small pink flowers, minutely spotted with red.
Height 25cm (10in).
Growing tips Rooting is easy from trailing stems though seed can be used.
Uses A component of snuff and used for headaches.

GLYCYRRHIZA GLABRA LIQUORICE

One of the most widely used medicinal plants, liquorice has been cultivated in England, since 1562, and taken to the New World the following century. Juice from the root system provides the commercial liquorice.

Features Leaflets that droop and long pods of hard seeds.
Colour Pale bluish-white pea-flowers.
Height 1.2m (4ft).
Growing tips Pieces of root can be planted in good sandy loam.
Uses Beverages, confectionery, coughs, bronchitis and gastric ulcers.

HAMAMELIS VIRGINIANA WITCH HAZEL

Graceful small deciduous tree with scented flowers in late autumn. Similar in appearance to the European hazel, the American hazel has seeds which are ejected with enough force to bombard passers-by.

Features Heavily veined leaves.
Colour Yellow flowers.
Height 3.6m (12ft).
Growing tips Best cultivated by layering in autumn. Grow in moist loam and light shade.
Uses For the treatment of bruises, sprains, varicose veins, inflammation, and as a skin tonic.

HUMULUS LUPULUS HOP

A twining plant, hop scrambles up hedges and posts quite naturally. Known universally as the most important ingredient in brewing beers, it is the dangling cone-like, green female flowers that are used. A splendid plant to introduce into a sunny herb garden.

Features Broad, rough vine leaves.
Colour Pale pink to white.
Height 2m (7ft).
Growing tips Propagate from seed, cuttings, or suckers in rich soil.
Uses Beer, insomnia, herbal tea, digestive aid, earache.

HYSSOPUS OFFICINALIS HYSSOP

A good hedging shrub with scented flowers which attract bees. Needs protection in severe winters and may need replacing every five years.

Features Aromatic leaves.
Colour Purple-blue, pink or white flowers.
Height 90cm (3ft).
Growing tips Root division or cuttings grown in light soil in a sunny position.
Uses Soups, casseroles and sausages. In Chartreuse liqueur. As medicine for coughs, sore throats, bronchitis. Pot pourri and insect repellant.

IBERIS AMARA CANDYTUFT

A tiny plant native to the British Isles on thin upland chalky soils, it is not widely cultivated in herb gardens. The tiny leaves are almost hidden by the flower heads. Rounded pods of seed follow which are used to make tinctures.

Features Good as an edging plant.
Colour Chalk-white flower heads.
Height 15cm (6in).
Growing tips Seed is sewn *in situ* in spring. Needs good drainage and an alkaline soil.
Uses Effective against rheumatism and fluid retention.

INULA HELENIUM ELECAMPANE

A statuesque hardy perennial, with very large basal leaves. Native to Europe and Asia, it is generally grown for medicinal purposes.

Features Aromatic roots which yield an oil which smells of bananas.
Colour Yellow daisy flowers from mid-summer.
Height 2m (7ft).
Growing tips Division of roots provides new stock which prefer a dampish soil.
Uses Culinary flavouring. Antiseptic oil used for bronchitis, catarrh and a skin wash.

IRIS FLORENTINA   FLORENTINE IRIS

One of the oldest hardy cultivated plants, native to southern Europe. Takes a while to establish itself as the knobbly rhizomes do not develop until the third year after planting.

Features Sword-shaped leaves.
Colour White, voilet-tinged flowers in early summer.
Height 75cm (30in).
Growing tips Divide rhizomes in late spring. Plant in rich soil in a sunny position.
Uses Purgative. Fragrant root in perfumery, pot pourri.

IRIS GERMANICA   ORRIS ROOT

Orris root is used in medicine. The bulbous and fleshy rhizome is white under the skin and smells strongly of violets. Prefer deep, fertile soil in full sun.

Features Sword-shaped leaves form a fan shape as they grow.
Colour White, tinged with mauve or with a yellow beard.
Height 90cm (3ft).
Growing tips Division of rhizomes in late spring. They should be planted half above and half below the soil.
Uses Fixative in pot pourri, in talcum powder, bath preparations.

IRIS PSEUDACORUS YELLOW IRIS

Also known as blue flag and sword flag, the yellow flag is a common plant of waterway borders and marshy ground in Great Britain. They can form extensive colonies and the leaves are sharp-edged.

Features Sword-shaped leaves.
Colour Yellow, violet, blue or white.
Height 1.5m (5ft).
Growing tips Can only be grown successfully as a water plant.
Uses The powdered root is an ingredient of snuff and a slice can cure toothache. Yellow dye from the flowers.

LAURUS NOBILIS BAY

One of the most versatile herbs and if regularly clipped, is one of the most decorative of shrubs. Can be clipped into neat topiary shapes and used decoratively on a porch or terrace.

Features Flat, pointed oval leaves.
Colour Small yellow insignificant flowers.
Height 7.5m (25ft).
Growing tips Propagation is by heel cuttings taken in summer
Uses In cooking and as a garnish. An infusion treats flatulence. Dried leaves are added to pot pourri.

LAVANDULA ANGUSTIFOLIA LAVENDER

This is a traditional cottage-garden plant, providing colour throughout the year. The flowers have many culinary, cosmetic and domestic used, and are a valuable ingredient of pot pourri.

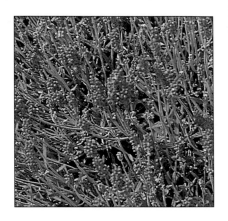

Features Grey-green spiky foliage which if unpruned become straggly.
Colour Mauvy-blue tubular flowers on long spikes.
Height 90cm (3ft).
Growing tips Take cuttings in spring. Likes dry, well-drained stony soil in a sunny position.
Uses Flavouring for fruit salads, candied, a rinse for clothes and hair.

LEONORUS CARDIACA MOTHERWORT

Introduced from Siberia in 1658, the plant found its way to America. Horizontally-growing underground stems support the stiff square flowers stalks.

Features Whole plant gives off an unpleasant smell.
Colour Tiny pink, spotted red flowers.
Height 1m (3ft).
Growing tips Once established will survive the hardiest winters in Europe. Good clumps form in a year or so.
Uses Heart stimulant, pulse regulatory action, menstrual regulator.

LEPTANDRA VIRGINICA BLACKROOT

Also known as Culver's Root or Culver's Physic. Used by Native Americans to clear bile and aid digestion. Native to eastern and southern America.

Features Long spikes of flowers and deeply lobed and pointed leaves.
Colour White flowers on long spikes.
Height 2m (7ft).
Growing tips Propagation by division of rhizomes in spring. Divide the clumps every three to four years.
Uses Rhizomes contain a volatile oil used to treat dysentry, enteritis and allied complaints.

LEVISTICUM OFFICINALE LOVAGE

Much used during the Middle Ages and then went out of fashion. It is the tallest of the umbellifers and makes an attractive back-of-the-border addition.

Features Celery-like aroma.
Colour Small yellow umbrella-like clusters.
Height 1.8m (6ft).
Growing tips Seed can be sewn outdoors or root cuttings propagated. Likes good, moist soil in partial shade.
Uses Leaves used in soups, casseroles, sauces and marinades. Candied stems as angelica and seeds flavour bread and crackers.

MARRUBIUM VULGARE WHITE OR COMMON HOREHOUND

Grown in many countries, it is square stemmed and fibrously tough with wrinkled leaves, blistered and hairy. An extract made from the crushed leaves is used in horehound pastilles and syrup, still made today.

Features Silky hairs give this plant a frosty appearance.
Colour Tiny white flowers in mid-summer.
Height 60cm (2ft).
Growing tips Loose, dry soil in a sunlit spot. Propagate by root division.
Uses Coughs and chest ailments, juice treats canker worm in trees, soaked leaves used as an insecticide.

MELISSA OFFICINALIS LEMON BALM

This plant has either yellow or variegated leaves smelling strongly of lemons. It is very attractive to bees and made a popular drink for Victorian ladies.

Features A vigorous grower that will readily spread through the border.
Colour Small white flowers.
Height 90cm (3ft).
Growing tips Grow in sunken pots to restrict growth. grow from seed or root division. Prefers moist, fertile soil and partial shade.
Uses Salads, cake decoration, garnish. Lemon peel substitute, skin toner.

MENTHA PULEGIUM PENNYROYAL

A herbaceous perennial and close relation of mint, Pennyroyal has a bitter taste many find unpleasant. It grows by prostrate stems creeping along the ground and forms dense ground cover.

Features Creeping habit with a strong pepermint scent.
Colour Purple flowers in tight clusters.
Spread 30cm (1ft).
Growing tips Plenty of moisture but will tolerate poor soil. Grow in full sun or partial shade.
Uses Used sparingly in place of mint. Relieves insect bites and stings, moth repellant, headaches and colds.

MENTHA SPICATA GARDEN MINT

Many species exist but spearmint is the most commonly grown domestic mint. Grows wild throughout northern Europe and will do so in a garden if not contained. The Romans introduced both spearmint and mint sauce to Britain.

Features Tough, vigorous roots which creep below ground to make new plants.
Colour Small bluish-mauve flowers on cylindrical spires.
Height 45cm (18in).
Growing tips Planting the runners in spring will produce more plants.
Uses Mint sauce, added to vegetables, garnish, mint tea, pot pourri.

NEPETA CATARIA CATMINT

This mint has few culinary uses, but is an attractive addition to a border. A herbaceous perennial, it is native to Asia and Europe and is loved by cats who roll on it.

Features Leaves resemble stinging nettles.
Colour Clusters of white or pale-blue flowers.
Height 90cm (3ft).
Growing tips Grow from seed, root division or cuttings in partial shade.
Uses Fresh leaves can be used in salads. A tisane of leaves and flowers can treat coughs, colds and catarrh.

OCYMUM BASILICUM SWEET BASIL

A popular windowsill plant and companion to tomatoes. The herb is a half-hardy annual. With adequate heat a plant will stay in leaf indoors right through to midwinter. It can be preserved in oil and salt or frozen.

Features Highly aromatic leaves.
Colour White, tubular flowers on spikes.
Height 60cm (2ft).
Growing tips Ideal for windowsills but will grow outdoors in a sheltered spot.
Uses Used to make *pesto* sauce, served with pasta or stirred into soup.

OENOTHERA BIENNIS EVENING PRIMROSE

This is an indigenous plant of America, used to treat nervous disorders and multiple scerosis. The essentail oil is considered important and is found in many health and toiletry products. It is also a cultivated garden plant, popular for its long flowering season.

Features Bedraggled appearance with delicately scented, floppy flowers.
Colour Pale yellow.
Height 1.5m (3ft).
Growing tips Well drained soil in a dry sunny corner.
Uses Astringent, essential oil, nerves, digestion.

ORIGANUM MAJORANA SWEET MARJORAM

This herb can be used in many ways for culinary use, flower arranging or pot pourri. Treat as a half-hardy annual as it will not survive severe winters. Inclined to be straggly with woody stems.

Features Highly perfumed and decorative herb.
Colour White, pale mauve or purple.
Height 25cm (10in).
Growing tips Moist, fertile soil in a sunny position.
Uses Leaves in casseroles, sauces, stuffings, egg and cheese dishes. Pot pourri, herbal sleep pillows.

ORIGANUM VULGARE OREGANO

A close relative of marjoram, oregano is an aromatic herb of southern Italy. Used mainly in its dried form, to flavour pizzas and tomato sauces. Used in Mexican chilli powder, this is a hardy annual with woody stems.

Features Retains its aroma when dried for a long time.
Colour White flowers on long spikes.
Height 60cm (2ft).
Growing tips Well-drained soil in full sun. Does well in indoor mini-propagators, place on windowsills.
Uses Salads, casseroles, sauces. With tomatoes, risotto beans and rice.

PAPAVER SOMNIFERUM OPIUM POPPY

An addictive and poisonous plant but unsurpassed as a sedative for pain relief. Flowers are sometime single, sometimes double, with petals looking like tissue paper balls.

Features Hardy, self-seeding annual.
Colour Mauve, white or pink flowers.
Height 1m (3ft).
Growing tips Seed should be sown afresh each spring in a sunny spot.
Uses Sedative of morphine and codeine. Seed decorates bread and used to thicken curries. Seed oil is used in the mixing of paints.

PELARGONIUM SCENTED LEAVED GERANIUM

One of the most useful herbs to have on your kitchen windowsill. They are ideal for growing indoors. Outside they are half-hardy and collapse at the first sign of frost.

Features Large shrubby, evergreen perennials with fragrant leaves.
Colour White, mauve pink or red flowers.
Height 90cm (3ft).
Growing tips Grown from tip cuttings in well-drained soil and plenty of sun.
Uses Infused in milk, cream and syrups for deserts. Used for garnishing.

PETROSELINUM CRISPUM PARSLEY

An invaluable addition to bouquets garni. With its frilled, curly leaves, it is one of the most widely used herbs for garnishing and for cooking. Italian flat leaved parsley is less decorative but is easier to grow and has a sharper flavour. It is biennial and self-seeds

Features Curly leaved or flat-leaved.
Colour Yellowish-green flowers.
Height 45cm (18in).
Growing tips Soaking the seed in warm water speeds up germination.
Uses As a garnish and in soups sauces and casseroles.

PHYTOLACCA AMERICANA POKEWEED

Indigenous to the warmer zones of America. Found on roadsides and wasteland, it has a reputation as a remedy for internal cancers. Damson purple berries provide a rich dye.

Features Young shoots may be eaten as asparagus, but as the roots mature, they become poisonous.
Colour Greenish-white flowers.
Height 2m (6ft).
Growing tips Plant in spring or autumn in moisture-retentive soil, in a sheltered area.
Uses Relieving headaches, rheumatism and arthritis.

PODOPHYLLUM PELTATUM AMERICAN MANDRAKE

A plant of shaded meadows and damp woodland. The fleshy roots yield a drug with a powerful action on the liver. Seen as a semi-aquatic plant in England, invaluable in bog and herb gardens.

Features Rich, red coloured leaves in late summer.
Colour Single white flowers.
Height 45cm (30in).
Growing tips Divide established clumps in spring.
Uses Fruit is edible, though acidic in flavour.

POLEMONIUM CAERULEM JACOB'S LADDER

A reasonably common decorative
garden perennial, flowering in
mid-summer. A hundred years ago it
was used as an anti-syphilitic agent and
as a treatment for rabies.

Features Hardy, herbaceous perennial.
Colour Deep, rich blue or white
flowers.
Height 60cm (2ft).
Growing tips Moisture-retentive soil
in sunshine encourages growth.
Uses The bitter roots are used as an
astringent and against snake bites.

POLYGALA MILKWORT

A really pretty little plant that forms
colonies, well suited to the front of the
border in a decorative herb garden.
From late spring to mid summer flowers
dance above the basal foliage. Roots
are small, knotted, twisted and grey.

Features Pretty, colony-forming plant.
Colour Deep blue flowers.
Height 30cm (1ft).
Growing tips Alkaline soil with
good drainage suit the plant best.
Uses Roots used in general tonics,
act as a mild laxative and relieve chest
congestion.

POLYGONATUM MULTIFLORUM SOLOMON'S SEAL

Traditionally cultivated for its creeping rootstock and used by battered wives of the 15th and 16th centuries for black eyes. For centuries it has been used as a cosmetic to clear freckles and as a skin tonic.

Features A striking plant with dangling, waxy bell flowers.
Colour White flowers.
Height 60cm (2ft).
Growing tips Light moisture retentive soil in partial shade.
Uses Tonic and astringent, pain relief for bruises and haemorrhoids, cosmetic.

POLYGONUM BISTORTA BISTORT

Snakeroot is another vernacular name for bistort, descriptive of the rhizomes, which are rich in tannin. Very good ground cover where it is a handsome plant.

Features Upstanding, oval folded eaves with flower spikes.
Colour Sugar pink or white flowers.
Height 50cm (21in).
Growing tips Happy in sun or shade, propagate by division or seed.
Uses Astringent. Pudding ingredient in northern England, salads.

PORTULACA OLERACEA PURSLANE

A plant taken to America by the settlers. The older leaves provided a green vegetable, the stems were pickled as a relish. A sprawling, succulent annual with reddish stems.

Features Leaves can be picked within six weeks of sowing.
Colour Tiny yellow flowers.
Height 15cm (6in).
Growing tips Sow seed when all frost has passed in a sunny position.
Uses Salads, sandwiches, coleslaw, garnish.

PRUNELLA VULGARIS SELF HEAL

An inhabitant of waste land, pasture and woodland verges, it is regarded as a persistent weed in many English gardens. It varies in height according to the conditions in which it grows and varies from ground-hugging spreading wed to an upstanding plant.

Features Barrel-shaped flower head.
Colour Mauve flowers and bracts.
Height 45cm (18in).
Growing tips Not common but a pink flowered form is available from some seed nurseries.
Uses An astringent, with honey for sore throats, mouthwash for ulcers.

PULMONARIA OFFICINALIS LUNGWORT

This plant has a fortifying action on the respiratory system and as it promotes perspiration, is used during influenza. Lungwort has been known in gardens in England for centuries. It has a cucumber flavour.

Features One of the earliest herbs to flower in the spring.
Colour Pink, mauve or blue according to the stage of development.
Height 30cm (1ft).
Growing tips Lightly shaded spot with moist, well-drained soil.
Uses As a pot herb, coughs, sore throats, congested tracts.

ROSA GALLICA OFFICINALIS ROSE

The 'apothecary's rose', the dried petals hold their fragrance and are widely used in the making of perfumes. The plant is a bush, thick and spreading. The leaves have five leaflets and the stems are thornless.

Features Strongly scented when dried.
Colour Bright red flowers.
Height 1.20m (4ft).
Growing tips Sunshine and moist soil are needed. Buy small plants as cuttings can be slow to take off.
Uses Candles, wine, vinegar, snuff, pot pourri, perfumes.

ROSMARINUS OFFICINALIS ROSEMARY

An evergreen shrub, rosemary is now available fresh year-round. Once dried, it loses much of its flavour. It is a pretty herb with long lasting flowers which are tubular in shape, carried on long spikes.

Features Slightly camphoric scent, tubular flowers
Colour Pale or bright blue flowers.
Height 2m (6ft).
Growing tips Grow from tip cuttings, taken in summer, in a sunny spot.
Uses With lamb, bouquets garni, in rice dishes, nerve tonic and antiseptic.

RUMEX SCUTATIS SORREL

Similar to spinach with lemony over-tones, a distinctive herb and vegetable. An herbaceous perennial, it has a variety of uses and is easy to grow. Best used young.

Features Spinach-like leaves.
Colour Greenish-red flowers.
Height 60cm (2ft).
Growing tips Seed is sewn outdoors in mid-spring, in moist, well-drained soil.
Uses Leaves cooked as a vegetable, salad, soup, casseroles, to curdle milk and make junket.

RUTA GRAVEOLENS RUE

Rue, is a sub-shrub known as the herb of grace, is a native of southern Europe where it flourishes in the poorest of soils. It makes a compact and decorative bush. The yellow flowers display well against the grey-green leaves. Later in the season it carries brown seedpods.

Features Bluish-green stems with bright yellow flowers.
Colour Bright yellow flowers.
Height 75cm (30in) high.
Growing tips Grow from seed or semi-hardwood cuttings in summer.
Uses Repels insects and used in flower arranging.

SALVIA OFFICINALIS SAGE

A decorative evergreen sub-shrub, though its leaves are not necessarily green. Some varieties have grey-green downy leaves. The flavour is very strong so only a little is used at any one time.

Features Strongly aromatic leaves.
Colour Grey-green.
Height 60cm (2ft).
Growing tips Thrives on poor, dry soil in a sunny spot.
Uses Sauces and stuffings for fatty meats and in sausages.

SALVIA OFFICINALIS PURPUREA RED SAGE

This is a purple-leaved form of the many varieties of sage. A decorative evergreen sub-shrub. The essential oil is very rich so only a little of the herb is used at any one time. The flavour and aroma can vary depending on which soil sage is planted in.

Features Decorative purple leaves.
Colour Purple leaves.
Height 90cm (3ft).
Growing tips Alkaline soil and a sunny position. Prune the plants well.
Uses Stuffings, cheeses, kebabs. Mouthwash and as a dentrifice.

SALVIA OFFICINALIS TRICOLOUR PAINTED SAGE

A daintier form of sage, where the young leaves are splashed with cream, pale green and cherry pink. This variety of sage is a less hardy plant and slow to establish itself. Requires well drained soil in sun.

Features Multi-coloured leaves.
Colour Cream, pale green and cherry pink leaves.
Height 90cm (3ft).
Growing tips Alkaline soil in a sunny area for this aromatic perennial.
Uses General tonic, fatty foods, gargle, hair rinse, antiseptic.

SALVIA SCLAREA CLARY SAGE

A close relation of sage, this is a decorative biennial that is usually treated as an annual. Introduced into Britain in the 16th century, when it was used in brewing and combined with elder flowers to give wine the flavour of muscatel.

Features Large wrinkled, darl leaves.
Colour Mauve with pink bracts.
Height 90cm (3ft).
Growing tips Grown from seed in spring, it will flower the following year. A light soil and warm sheltered position.
Uses Added to soups, casseroles beer and wines. Gargle and skin cleanser.

SAMBUSCUS NIGRA ELDER

Common throughout Europe, the elder has attracted a strong folk history. It was believed to keep witches at bay. Minute flowers, highly fragrant, are followed by purplish-black berries which hang in heavy trusses.

Features Umbrella-like, fragrant flowers.
Colour Creamy-white flowers.
Height 10m (30ft).
Growing tips Moist soil and plenty of sun needed to develop the fragrance.
Uses Flavouring fruit compotes, salads, gelatin puddings. Jams and jellies.

SANGUIARIA CANADENSIS BLOODROOT

A spring flowering perennial, bloodroot is native to North America. The bark of the root was used by Native Americans to dye themselves, and the root itself is a narcotic.

Features Dramatic leaves and a solitary flower.
Colour Pure white and waxy flower.
Height 30cm (1ft).
Growing tips Rich, moist soil in partial shade.
Uses High blood pressure, ringworm, eczema and ulcers. Thick, fleshy, root yields a deep orange/brown juice.

SATUREJA HORTENSIS SUMMER SAVOURY

A half-hardy annual that self-seeds freely, and has a hot and slightly bitter flavour reminiscent of thyme. The plant has an untidy, straggling habit with leaves that are long, narrow, and resemble soft pine needles.

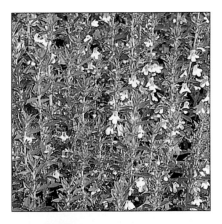

Features Pine-needle-like leaves.
Colour Pale mauve flowers.
Height 45cm (18in).
Growing tips Grown from seed in late spring, in a sheltered spot.
Uses With pork and game, soups pates, bouquets garnis, peas and beans. Tonic, easing stings and bites.

SATUREJA MONTANA   WINTER SAVOURY

A shrubby perennial with a similar though stronger, flavour to Summer Savoury, that was at one time frequently used with trout and other oily fish. The flowers are borne in spiky clusters. The leaves can be used sparingly with vegetables, especially beans and peas.

Features Greyish green leaves.
Colour Pinky white or pink flowers.
Height 30cm (1ft).
Growing tips Grown from seed in late summer, in warm soil in plenty of sun.
Uses The stronger flavour is considered inferior to Summer Savoury but the uses are similar.

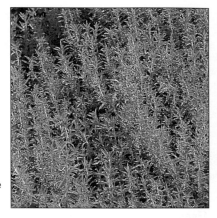

SMYRNIUM OLUSTRUM   ALEXANDERS

An ancient pot herb that grows wild in southern and western coastal areas of the British Isles. A hefty, handsome plant, particularly in spring before most other herbs are ready for use. It gives a good celery and parsley flavour.

Features Fragrant flowers and shiny, deeply divided leaves.
Colour White-green flowers.
Height 1.2m (4ft).
Growing tips Sow seed in mid-summer in an open position.
Uses Leaves in coleslaw, flavouring soups and stews.

SYMPHYTUM OFFICINALE COMFREY

In medieval times this herb was seen as a cure-all. Its country name of 'knit-bone', derives from application of ground root to broken joints, to produce a plaster-like effect. A perennial plant with no aroma and flowers that hang in clusters.

Features Bell-shaped flowers.
Colour Cream flashed with red.
Height 90cm (3ft).
Growing tips One plant is all that is needed to produce a patch of comfrey.
Uses Cooked and eaten as spinach. Cleansing skin oil. Pale yellow dye from leaves and stalks.

TANACETUM VULGARE TANSY

Native to Europe, tansy grows wild in the America. It was a common cottage-garden herb in medieval times, when it was used as an insect repellant, and a source of orange dye. A large and graceful plant with umbel like clusters of dome-shaped, attractive flowers.

Features Feathery pungent leaves.
Colour Bright, deep yellow flowers.
Height 90cm (3ft).
Growing tips Herbaceous perennial, grown by root division in dry, well-drained soil.
Uses Salads, egg dishes, dried flower arranging, insect repellant.

TARAXACUM OFFICINALE DANDELION

A herbaceous perennial that has become a rampant weed. The plant has a persistent root system that is difficult to eradicate. The flowers are made up of a mass of florets which when gone to seed, were part of a children's game.

Features Seeds form a fluffy ball, known as a 'clock'.
Colour Yellow.
Height 30cm (1ft).
Growing tips A piece of root will ensure dandelions forever.
Uses Medicinal use for all urinary troubles. Leaves in salads, cooked like spinach, wine and beer.

THYMUS VULGARIS GARDEN THYME

Thyme is a sun-loving herb, at its best when grown wild. In gardens, it will be less aromatic. A decorative herb, covered for two or three months with delicate, highly fragrant flowers, attractive to bees. There are many different species offering a range of flavours.

Features Highly fragrant flowers.
Colour Pale mauve flowers.
Height 20cm (8in).
Growing tips Likes poor, stony soil in full sun.
Uses Stuffings, bouquets garni, soups and casseroles. Antiseptic, pot pourri.

URTICA DIOICA NETTLE

A vigorous and rampant weed, very attractive to bees and butterflies and often grown for this reason. The leaves are dull green, sharp-toothed and the flowers are carried in curving trusses.

Features Hairy leaves which, when touched, leave formic acid and a burning sensation on the skin.
Colour Greenish-yellow flowers.
Height 1.8m (6ft).
Growing tips No one ever plants nettles: they just arrive and stay.
Uses Cooked like spinach, as soup, to make beer. Treatment of rheumatism, and as a diuretic.

VERBASCUM THAPSUS MULLEIN

One of the tallest and most attractive plants in the border, with its tall, stately spires of flowers. The flowers can be 30cm (12in) long. The plant has a long association with witchcraft and was a familiar plant in cottage gardens.

Features Woolly, grey green leaves.
Colour Pale yellow flowers.
Height 2m (6ft).
Growing tips A biennial, grown from seed in well-drained soil, in sun.
Uses No culinary uses. Leaves were used to treat coughs. A flower infusion is used to lighten hair, after straining to remove the minute hairs.

VERBENA OFFICINALIS VERVAIN

This herb grows wild on waste ground and by the wayside in Europe and North America. It has no culinary uses but a long history of medicinal applications, particularly in nervous disorders.

Features Hairy branching stems.
Colour Small mauve flowers.
Height 90cm (3ft).
Growing tips Grown from seed or from tip cuttings. Likes plenty of sun.
Uses Mild sedative, alleviate depression and aid digestion. A diluted infusion used to sooth sore eyes.

VALERIANA OFFICINALIS VALERIAN

A herb which is indifferent to the soil conditions in which it grows. Roots are lifted in the second and third year in the autumn. If grown for its root, the flowering stems are removed to encourage the rhizome to grow.

Features Tall herb with dark, ferny leaves at the base.
Colour Pink or white clusters of flowers.
Height 1.5m (5ft).
Growing tips Plant in moisture retentive soil.
Uses Painkiller and nervine, used in nervous disorders and for insomnia.

Index
Alphabetical listing of botanical names.

INDEX

Index
Alphabetical listing of common names.

I N D E X